Eva Wiechmann

Pursenality
PLUS

20 New Felted Bags

Martingale®
& COMPANY

Credits

President · *Nancy J. Martin*
CEO · *Daniel J. Martin*
VP and General Manager · *Tom Wierzbicki*
Publisher · *Jane Hamada*
Editorial Director · *Mary V. Green*
Managing Editor · *Tina Cook*
Technical Editor · *Darilyn Page*
Copy Editor · *Liz McGehee*
Design Director · *Stan Green*
Illustrator and Photo Stylist · *Robin Strobel*
Cover and Text Designer · *Trina Craig*
Photographer · *Brent Kane*

Dedication

To all the goodness in the world

Acknowledgments

Thank you to:

My husband for helping with a challenging computer problem. I also appreciate his patience for the "wet dogs" in the house—we had an unusually rainy season during the production of these bags—and for not complaining about all the take-out dinners.

The staff at Cascade Yarns for their support and enthusiasm. It made the work really fun.

My store "helpers," who had to explain to the customers why I wasn't there.

My customers, for your continuing support and your enthusiasm for the store and our books.

The friendly staff at Martingale & Company. It's been a privilege getting to know you. I'd like to express a very special thanks to Terry Martin for her help. I'd also like to thank Darilyn Page and Tina Cook for keeping me on track.

Last but not least, speical thanks to Robin Strobel and Brent Kane for the awesome illustrations and photos.

Pursenality Plus: 20 New Felted Bags
© 2006 by Eva Wiechmann

Martingale & Company
20205 144th Avenue NE
Woodinville, WA 98072-8478 USA
www.martingale-pub.com

Printed in China
11 10 09 08 07 06   8 7 6 5 4 3 2 1

Mission Statement

Dedicated to providing quality products
and service to inspire creativity.

Library of Congress Cataloging-in-Publication Data

Wiechmann, Eva.
    Pursenality plus : 20 new felted bags / Eva Wiechmann.
       p.   cm.
    ISBN 1-56477-653-0
1. Handbags.   2. Tote bags.   3. Felting.   I. Title.
    TT667.W45 2006
    646.4'8—dc22
                                        2005022843

Contents

Introduction

When I wrote *Pursenalities,* I hoped you would enjoy the patterns, but there was no way I could have anticipated the volume of positive comments I received. The requests for additional patterns and your favorable responses encouraged me to write *Pursenality Plus.*

The patterns in this book are practical and functional, but still fun and easy. *Pursenality Plus* includes 20 felted bags and totes with add-on embellishments that take felting to a new level. Purse handles, metal rings, grommets, eyelets, snaps, and buckles give the designs a professional look. You'll learn how to make felted flowers to adorn your bags, and you'll find useful accessories—including a cosmetics pouch, an eyeglasses case, and a cell phone holder—in the collection.

—Eva

Getting Started

Y OU'LL NEED BASIC knitting supplies and worsted-weight wool that isn't Superwash wool, plus some novelty yarns. For some bags, you'll also need a hammer and pliers, plus grommet and snap tools. A washing machine is an important part of the production of these bags. If you have a front-loading washing machine, refer to the manufacturer's instructions for information on how to stop the wash cycle before it goes into the rinse and spin cycles. You can felt items without a washing machine, but the process requires physical labor (see "Felting by Hand" on page 6).

Yarn

Cascade 220, a 100% wool that isn't a Superwash wool, is used extensively in this book. It's my favorite yarn for felting, but I use other wool yarns as well.

Note: *Remember, don't use a Superwash wool yarn for felting projects. Superwash wool yarns won't felt. When in doubt, try felting a small sample so you don't waste yarn and time on something that won't turn out the way you want.*

Felting

Felting is where the fun begins. It isn't difficult; just follow the directions in this section for felting in the washing machine or felting by hand.

Felting in a Washing Machine
To felt in a washing machine, follow these steps.

1. **Put the bag in a mesh garment bag or a zippered pillowcase.** Put each piece in a separate bag to prevent them from sticking together and to keep lint from clogging the washing machine.

2. **Set your machine for the regular wash cycle with hot water.** Add some nonrinse wool wash, such as Eucalan. The wool wash speeds the felting process and prevents some of the wet-dog

*The same project,
before and after felting*

odor you usually get from wet wool. Just a little spoonful is enough.

3. **Turn on the machine.** It's the agitation during the wash cycle, not just the hot water, that makes the fibers felt. Don't let the machine get to the rinse and spin cycles. Rinsing and spinning might leave permanent creases in your bag.

   Note: *When felting a bag with many colors or with a combination of light and dark colors, include a Shout Color Catcher sheet or a similar dye-absorbing product in the washing machine. Avoid letting the bag sit in standing water for a long time, because doing so may also cause discoloration.*

4. **Check the bag frequently.** It's important to take the bag out of the water and shape it throughout the felting process. To do this, stop the machine and pull the bag out of the water. Pull on the handles and straighten out the flap and corners. Pull on the bag to change the length and the width. Keep in mind that the knitting will felt more in height than in width, so sometimes you'll need to pull really hard to attain the desired shape.

   Keep felting long enough to create a firm fabric. This may require you to reset the machine to the wash cycle more than once. Individual stitches won't be visible in a bag that has been felted enough. A purse made with firm material will retain its shape during use.

5. **When you're satisfied that the bag is properly felted, squeeze out some of the water by hand.** Put the bag between towels and step on it to get out most of the water.

6. **Shape the bag again.** Think of it as dough that you can mold and tuck and pull. Use cardboard pieces to keep straight lines even. Stuff the bag with paper to get the shape you want.

7. **Air-dry the bag.** On a sunny day, you can hang it by the handles out in the open. If it's raining, the laundry room or garage will have to do. Keep shaping the purse as needed and let it dry completely.

8. **Shave the bag.** I shave my purses and bags to keep the colors looking crisp and the bags from shedding on my clothes. Inexpensive, disposable razors do a great job of removing fuzz. Shave the bags lightly, being careful not to cut the fabric. Battery-operated garment shavers also work well.

Felting by Hand

You can felt knitted projects by hand, but the process is more labor-intensive than felting in a washing machine. You'll need a large bucket, hot water, and a new, unused drain plunger. Pour hot water in the bucket, add some wool wash (such as Eucalan), put the bag in the bucket, and start plunging. Felting by hand takes a while, but it works. Keep checking the bag as you plunge to see how the felting is progressing.

Finished Sizes after Felting

All measurements are approximate. The finished size of your project depends on the fiber combinations, the colors of the yarns, and how tightly or loosely you knit. The finished size also depends on the shaping you did during the felting process.

Knitting Basics

MAKING A FELTED bag isn't complicated. A few easy knitting techniques are all you need.

Gauge

Gauge isn't too important. An approximate gauge of 2 to 2½ stitches per inch is fine. Loose is better than tight.

Stitches

The projects in this book are made with basic stitches. Note that they're worked differently, depending on whether you're working back and forth or in the round.

Garter Stitch (garter st)
Back and forth: Knit every row.
In the round: Knit 1 round, purl 1 round.

Stockinette Stitch (St st)
Back and forth: Knit 1 row, purl 1 row.
In the round: Knit every round.

Reverse Stockinette Stitch (rev St st)
Back and forth: Purl 1 row, knit 1 row.
In the round: Purl every round.

Increases

Increase (inc)
Knit into the back and front of the same stitch.

Make 1 (M1)
Pick up the horizontal thread between 2 stitches and knit into the back of it.

I-Cord

Many of the bags in this book use I-cord for handles, drawstrings, ties, and trim. Each project gives specific instructions for making these items, but the following explains the general technique.

With double-pointed needles (dpn), cast on the required number of stitches as indicated in the pattern. *Do not turn.* Push the stitches to the opposite end of the needle and knit across. Repeat until you have the length needed. Bind off.

To join the ends of handles, graft the cast-on end to the bound-off stitches. Thread a tapestry needle with yarn; insert the needle inside the cast-on edge and then into the corresponding stitch on the bound-off edge. Continue around.

To make an I-cord in reverse stockinette stitch, purl all the stitches. This method is used in the Eyeglasses Case on page 58.

One-Row Buttonholes

One-row buttonholes are used for the pocket openings for many of the projects in this book and for handles in the All in One and Roses Are Red purses.

Knit to the buttonhole (or pocket) placement. With the yarn in front, slip the next 2 stitches purlwise, bind off 1 stitch; *slip the next stitch purlwise and bind off*. Repeat from * to * as many times as needed for the opening. Slide the last stitch back to the left-hand needle, turn, use the needle CO (see "Needle Cast On" on page 9) to cast on the number of stitches required in the pattern, turn. Continue following the pattern instructions.

Kitchener Stitch

This is a way to join two pieces of knitting without leaving a visible seam. With the same number of stitches on two needles, hold the wrong sides together and work the stitches with a tapestry needle as follows:

1. With yarn threaded on a tapestry needle, go through the first stitch on the front needle purlwise; leave the stitch on the needle.

2. Go through the first stitch on the back needle knitwise; leave the stitch on the needle.

3. Go through the first stitch on the front needle knitwise; drop this stitch off the needle. Go through the next stitch on the front needle purlwise; leave it on the needle.

4. Go through the first stitch on the back needle purlwise; take it off the needle. Go through the second stitch of the back needle knitwise; leave the stitch on the needle.

5. Repeat steps 3 and 4 until there is 1 stitch on each needle.

6. Go through the last stitch on the front needle knitwise; drop the stitch off.

7. Go through the last stitch on the back needle purlwise; drop the stitch off. Weave in the end.

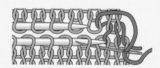

Three-Needle Bind Off

This technique is used to join the bottom edges in some of the bags. Divide the stitches evenly onto 2 needles and hold the needles with the right sides together. With a third needle, knit together 1 stitch from the front needle and 1 stitch from the back needle. *Knit together the next stitch on the front and back needles. With 2 stitches on your right needle, bind off by pulling the first stitch over the second stitch and off the needle.* Repeat from * to * until all the stitches are bound off.

Note: *When using a circular needle, you can just hold the tips in one hand and bind off with a separate needle. Pull the loop end through the middle of the stitches. There is no need to transfer to a different needle.*

Knit together 1 stitch
from front needle and
1 stitch from back needle.

Bind off.

Needle Cast On

Knit into the stitch on the left needle; don't take it off the needle. Put the new stitch back on the left needle. Repeat from * to * for the required number of stitches.

Knit into stitch.   Place new stitch on left needle.

Provisional Cast On

With waste yarn, crochet a loose chain for the required number of stitches plus a few extra. One way to ensure a loose chain is to crochet over the top of a knitting needle, then with a needle and the main yarn, pick up the required number of stitches from the back of the chain. Knit the stitches according to the pattern. The waste yarn will be removed later to release the stitches.

Crochet a chain over top of knitting needle.

Remove chain 1 stitch at a time.

Single Crochet

Work from right to left with the right side facing you. *Insert the crochet hook into the next stitch, yarn over the hook and pull up a loop, yarn over the hook and pull through the 2 loops on the hook.* Repeat from * to *.

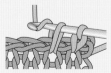

Insert hook into stitch, yarn over hook, pull loop through to front, yarn over hook.

Pull loop through both loops on hook.

Tuck Stitch

This stitch is used to create a gathered, tubelike pattern, such as the one used in the Tutu purse.

Work the required number of rows, ending with a completed wrong-side row. *With a double-pointed needle, pick up the required number of stitches from the purl side (the pattern will specify which row to pick up), leaving all of the stitches on the needle. Move all the stitches to the right-hand end of the needle and hold the double-pointed needle parallel with the left-hand needle that contains the live stitches. With a third needle, *knit 1 stitch from the front needle and 1 stitch from the back needle together.* Repeat from * to * for as many stitches as are on the double-pointed needle.

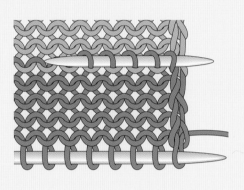

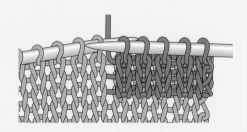

Double Decrease

Slip 2 stitches knitwise, knit 1, pass the 2 slipped stitches over the knit stitch.

Adding Beads to a Bag

Slip a stitch off the needle. With a crochet hook, pull the stitch though a bead and then put this stitch back on your left-hand needle and knit the stitch. This method works for beads with large holes, such as pony beads.

Attaching Handles to the Bags

Each pattern in this book provides instructions for attaching the handles to the bags. Several patterns call for the use of grommets and snaps. Since there are different types of grommets and snaps, we suggest you read and follow the manufacturer's instructions for the products you use (see "Resources" on page 63 for the sources of products used in this book).

Attaching Rings

Rings are used to attach handles to some projects. O rings are used in Black-Tie Affair (page 54). D rings are used in Jackie O (page 44) and in the Cell Phone Holder (page 60).

- Knit or purl to the placement of the ring. Place the ring over the right-hand needle.

- Knit or purl the number of stitches specified in the pattern. Then flip the ring over the last stitch on the right-hand needle and work the remainder of the row as established.

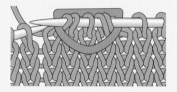

Zippers

Zippers are used in three projects: Iris (page 32), Mrs. Watson (page 36) and the Cosmetics Pouch (page 56). The materials list indicates the zipper size required for the project. If you can't find the exact size needed, or if you find that your bag ended up slightly smaller than expected after felting, you can easily shorten a too-long zipper. To shorten, tightly whipstitch across

the top of the teeth 8 to 10 times with a double strand of sewing thread. Cut the zipper ½" above the whipstitches. Sew the zipper in place using a Sharp sewing needle and sewing thread.

Seams

All seams are joined with a whipstitch using 1 or 2 strands of wool and a tapestry needle. Use the same number of strands that were used for the bag that you're seaming.

Pockets

Most of the purses in this book have pockets that are felted separately and sewn on after all pieces are completely dry. Use perle cotton or embroidery floss and an embroidery needle to sew the pocket onto the bag. Use a whipstitch and all 6 strands of the floss. Pocket linings are sewn after felting, using perle cotton or floss and an embroidery needle.

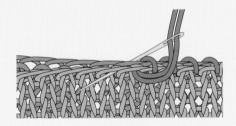

Whipstitch

Purse Bottom Insert

Purse bottom inserts help the bags with flat bottoms keep their shape during use. These inserts are optional.

To make an insert for a bag, use heavyweight cardboard and cut a shape that will fit comfortably in the bottom of the bag. A rectangular shape works well in most bags, but you may be creative and make any shape you like.

Cut two pieces of fabric the same size as the cardboard plus a ¼" seam allowance on three sides and a 2" allowance at one end. With the right sides of the fabric facing each other, sew around the seam allowance on three sides, leaving the side with the 2" allowance unsewn. Turn the fabric cover inside out so the right side is facing out. Place the cardboard inside the cover and fold under the open end of the cover.

Place the covered insert into the bottom of the bag. The insert can be removed easily to be cleaned or changed as desired.

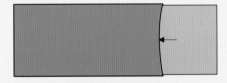

Felted Flowers

Winter

Spring

Summer

Fall

*F*lowers reflect the season and can add a touch of color to any bag. The flowers you make are limited only by your imagination and the colors of the yarns you have on hand. Use these basic instructions as a starting point for your own creativity. You may use any shape or size petals and add leaves and stems to your creations as you wish. Have fun and see where your mind takes you.

Materials

- Cascade 220 (100% wool; 220 yards) in a variety of colors
- Size 11 US (8 mm) needles
- Thread for sewing
- Sharp needle
- Jewelry pin

Skill Level: Beginner

Flower

- With 1 strand of Cascade, CO 30 sts. Work St st for approximately 8". You can knit different colors all together into a long scarf.

- Felt the scarf into a firm fabric (see "Felting" on pages 5–6). Let dry.

- With scissors or pinking shears, cut out the petals and leaves. Cut 1 long, narrow piece for the center.

- Arrange the pieces in a circle, with either the points or the rounded ends in the center, according to the look you want. Using the needle and thread, stitch the pieces together at the center. Coil the centerpiece, and stitch it to the center of the flower. Then stitch the leaves to the underside of the flower. Stitch several times through all the layers to stabilize the flower.

- Sew the pin to the back.

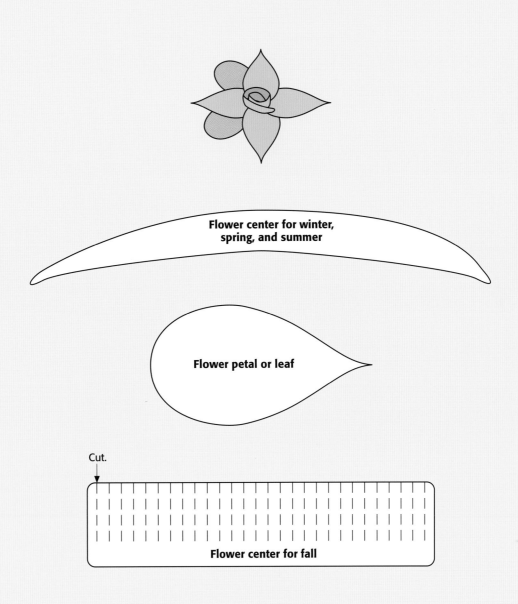

Flower center for winter, spring, and summer

Flower petal or leaf

Cut.

Flower center for fall

Tutu

When Cascade Yarns introduced two new pink colors to their yarn line, this lovely bag came to my mind. The bag is playful and a little frilly, like a ballerina's dress.

Materials

- Cascade 220 (100% wool; 220 yards) **[4]**
  - **MC**   2 skeins of Light Pink (color 4192)
  - **CC1**   2 skeins of Dark Pink (color 9478)
  - **CC2**   2 skeins of Medium Pink (color 9477)
- Size 15 US (10 mm) circular needle (24")
- Size 17 US (12 mm) needles
- Stitch holder
- Stitch marker
- One 1¼"-long rectangular button and four ¾"-long rectangular buttons
- 24" length of ⅜"-wide pink ribbon
- Sewing needle and thread

Skill Level: Intermediate

Finished Size after Felting:
Approx 14½" wide x 9" high

Note: *Beg bag at bottom. Work 2 strands of yarn held tog throughout.*

Bag

- With size 17 needles and 1 strand each of MC and CC2 held tog, CO 30 sts.
- *Work 8 rows in St st.
- Work tuck stitch for 5 sts (knit each of the 5 sts tog with sts picked up from 5 rows below the current row on the purl side), knit to last 5 sts, work tuck stitch on last 5 sts (see "Tuck Stitch" on page 9).
- Purl 1 row.* Rep from * to * 8 more times. BO all sts.

Front and Back
- With size 15 needle and 2 strands of CC1, PU 39 sts along the side with the tuck sts. Mark center st. Purl 1 row.
- **Dec row:** Sl 1, K1, psso, knit to 1 st before center st, work double decrease (see "Double Decrease" on page 9), knit to end.
- **Next rnd:** Sl 1, P1, psso, purl to end. Rep last 2 rows until 3 sts rem. BO.
- Work back the same as front.

Top Edge
- With size 15 needle and 2 strands of CC1, PU 28 sts, beg from right corner of bottom edge, PU 35 sts from front edge, PU 28 sts from left top, PU 35 sts from back, PM—126 sts.
- **Dec rnd:** *(K2tog) 14 times, K35,* rep from * to * once—98 sts.
- Purl 3 rnds.
- P14, BO 35 sts, P14 (put on holder), BO 35 sts.

Handle

- With size 15 needle and 2 strands of CC1, work 12 rows in rev St st (slipping first st as if to purl on each row) on rem 14 sts.
- **Dec row:** Sl 1, P4, (P2tog) twice, P5—12 sts.
- Cont rev St st on 12 sts for 19".
- **Inc row:** Sl 1, K4, inc in next 2 sts, K5—14 sts.
- Work 12 more rows. Join with kitchener stitch to sts on holder (see "Kitchener Stitch" on page 8).

Flap

- With RS facing, size 15 needle, and 2 strands of CC1, PU 37 sts from third purl row of back. Work 5 rows in St st, keeping first 2 sts and last 2 sts in garter st.
- **Inc rnd:** With size 17 needles and CC2, knit in front and back of each stitch across—74 sts.
- Work St st for 7 rows.
- **Dec rnd:** Knit first 2 sts and last 2 sts tog EOR 6 times. BO rem sts—62 sts.

Finishing

- Felt bag according to instructions (see "Felting" on pages 5–6). Pinch ruffle to keep shape and let handle curl at top.
- Tie ribbon bow inside, creating loop for large button. Sew button to outside.
- Sew 4 small buttons on top of flap. Lace ribbon around buttons for decoration and tack in place.

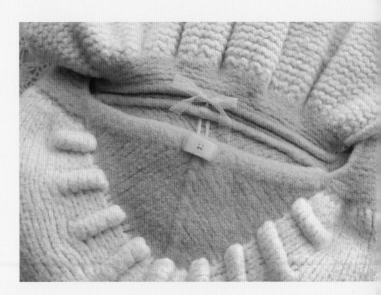

Blue Sky

There's something so sweet and innocent about baby blue and white. This bag brings to mind a spring sky with patchy white clouds.

Materials

- Cascade 220 (100% wool; 220 yards) [4]
    - **MC** 3 skeins of Light Blue (color 7815)
    - **CC** 1 skein of White (color 8505)
- Size 15 US (10 mm) circular needle (24")
- Size 11 US (8 mm) circular needle (24")
- Size 11 US (8 mm) double-pointed needles
- 2 heavy-duty silver snaps
- 4 stitch holders
- Stitch marker
- Perle cotton or embroidery floss and embroidery needle

Skill Level: Intermediate

Finished Size after Felting: Approx 10" wide x 7" high x 2¼" deep (excluding the trim)

Note: *Beg bag at bottom. Work 2 strands of yarn held tog throughout unless otherwise indicated.*

Bag

- With MC and size 15 needle, CO 30 sts. Knit 1 row. Work 18 rows in St st, beg with knit row.
- Knit 2 rows.
- PU 15 sts from a short end, PU 30 sts from next long end, PU 15 stitches from next short end, PM—90 sts.
- Work in rnds: (K30, P15) twice for 12".
- **Dec rnd:** * (K4, K2tog) 5 times, (P3, P2tog) 3 times*, rep from * to * once—74 sts.
- Change to size 11 circular needle. Purl 1 rnd.

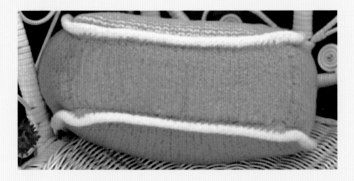

Top Tabs

Snaps are added to these tabs to close top of bag.

- Cont with size 11 needle and 2 strands of MC, BO 17 pw, P5 (put these sts on holder), BO 5 sts, P5 (put these sts on holder), BO 22 sts, P5 (put these sts on holder), BO 5 sts, P5 (put these sts on holder), BO 5 sts.
- *Join yarn to sts on holder, work 14 rows in St st, BO.* Rep from * to * 4 times.

Handles and Trim (Make 2)

The handles and trim are worked in 1 piece.

- With dpn and 1 strand of CC, CO 4 sts. Work 4-st I-cord for 26" (see "I-Cord" on page 8). This makes the handle.

- **Dec:** K1, K2tog, K1. Cont with 3-st I-cord for approx 24" to go around sides and bottom. This makes the trim.

Note: *Before you finish off, start stitching trim with 1 strand of Cascade around bag to see if you have correct length.*

- Join end of bag trim to end of handle just above top.
- Tie 2 strands of MC around handles, leaving a short tail for a funky finish. Rep about every 2" along both handles.

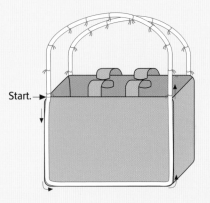

Start. →

Pocket

With size 15 needle and 2 strands of MC, CO 30 sts. Work St st as follows: Purl 1 row. (Work 1 row CC, 1 row MC) 6 times, (work 2 rows CC, 2 rows MC) 3 times. With size 11 needle, work 4 rows in garter st. BO.

Finishing

- Felt bag and pocket according to instructions (see "Felting" on pages 5–6).
- Sew pocket to outside of bag.
- Attach snaps to tabs, following manufacturer's instructions.

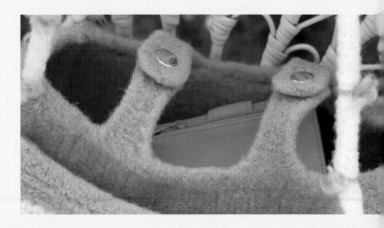

Little Giant

The name says it all. Pull the drawstrings tight for a compact bag, or extend them when you need more room. The versatility of this bag will make it one of your favorites.

Materials

- Nature Wool (100% wool; 240 yards) **4**
  - **MC** 2 skeins of Spring Green (color 32)
- Cascade 220 (100% wool; 220 yards) **4**
  - **CC1** 1 skein of Heather Green (color 9461)
- Di.Ve' Black Jack (100% polyamide, 76 yards) **3**
  - **CC2** 1 ball of Green (color 355)
- Madil Kid Seta (70% kid mohair, 30% silk; 230 yards) **1**
  - **CC3** 1 ball of Chartreuse (color 725)
    - 1 ball of Teal (color 403) for flowers on front
- Size 15 US (10 mm) circular needle (24")

- Size 13 US (9 mm) double-pointed needles
- Size 11 US (8 mm) double-pointed needles
- Stitch marker
- Grommet kit and hammer
- 4 large grommets, 7/16"
- 16 medium grommets, 1/2"
- 4 purse-strap crimps, 1/2" long
- 2 pieces of 3/8"-diameter PVC tubing, each approx 12" long
- Sewing needle and thread
- Tapestry needle

Skill Level: Easy

Finished Size after Felting:
Approx 12" wide x 12" high

Note: *Beg bag at bottom. Work with 2 strands of yarn held tog unless otherwise indicated.*

Bag

- With size 15 circular needle and 2 strands of CC1, CO 90 sts and join into rnd, PM. Knit 8 rnds.
- Drop 1 strand of CC1 and add 1 strand of MC, knit 4 rnds.
- Cut CC1 and add another strand of MC. Cont with 2 strands of MC until piece measures 13" from beg.
- Cut 1 strand of MC, add 1 strand of CC1, and knit 4 rnds.
- Drop MC. With 2 strands of CC1, knit 8 rnds.
- **Dec rnd:** (K8, K2tog) around—81 sts.
- Add 1 strand of CC2 to 2 strands of CC1. Purl 3 rnds. BO pw.

Handles (Make 2)

- With 2 strands of CC1 and size 13 dpn, CO 5 sts. (Sl 1, K4, turn) for 9".
- Cont on 5 sts, working 5-st I-cord for 14" (see "I-Cord" on page 8).
- End by working (sl 1, K4, turn) for 9". BO.

Drawstrings

With size 11 dpn and 1 strand of CC1, CO 3 sts. Work 3-st I-cord for 64" (see "I-Cord" on page 8). You'll cut this length in half after felting.

Finishing

Different grommets and grommet kits are available. Follow the manufacturer's instructions for the grommets you purchase. Refer to the project photos for placement.

- Insert 2 large $^7/_{16}$" grommets on each side of the purse 7 to 8 sts from sides under top trim.
- Attach 16 medium grommets to sides. Place grommets 3 sts and 12 rows apart, beg 10 rows from bottom. There are 8 grommets on the front and 8 on the back of the bag.
- Insert PVC tubing into I-cord section of handle. Using sewing thread and a sharp needle, tack down to prevent the tubing from escaping during the felting process. Make sure to sew right through the tubing.
- Fold flat ends of handle through large grommets at top of bag and whipstitch with CC1 to beg of I-cord.
- Felt bag and drawstrings according to instructions (see "Felting" on pages 5–6).
- The drawstrings are threaded through the medium grommets down the side of the bag. Removing or loosening these drawstrings allows the bag to expand. Cut I-cord for drawstrings in half; attach crimps to ends. Lace from the top down on each side. The sides can be tall or pulled up for a funky, gathered effect.
- With 2 shades of Kid Seta held tog, use tapestry needle to embroider lazy-daisy flowers to the front.

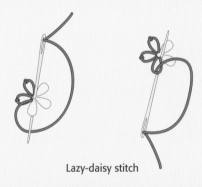

Lazy-daisy stitch

Purple Haze

When I was working on this bag, the radio station played the song "Purple Haze" by Jimi Hendrix. The song captured the originality and fun personality of this bag.

Materials

- Cascade 220 (100% wool; 220 yards) 🧶**4**
  - **MC** 4 skeins of Lite Lavender (color 7809)
  - **CC** 1 skein of Medium Lavender (color 8888)
- 1 ball of Crystal Palace Fizz Stardust (86% poly, 14% Lurex; 120 yards) (color 4197) 🧶**4**
- Size 15 US (10 mm) circular needle (24")
- Size 11 US (8 mm) circular needle (24")

- Size 13 double-pointed needles
- Size I (6 mm) crochet hook
- Stitch marker
- 2 D-ring clamps, small (1¼")
- 2 glass buttons, 1" wide
- 2 magnetic snaps, 9/16"
- 2 pieces (12 links each) of ⅜"-wide silver chain
- Tapestry needle

Skill Level: Intermediate

Finished Size after Felting:
Approx 14" wide x 6½" high x 4½" deep

Note: *Beg bag at bottom. Work 2 strands of yarn held tog throughout.*

Bag

- With size 15 needle and 2 strands of CC, CO 38 sts. Knit 1 row. Cont in St st, beg with knit row, for 26 rows. Knit 2 rows. Cut CC.
- With MC, knit across 38 sts, PU 24 sts from short end, PU 38 sts from opposite side, PU 24 sts from next short end, PM—128 sts. Purl 1 rnd.
- **Inc rnd:** (K38, inc in each of next 24 sts by knitting in front and back of stitch) twice.
- **Next rnd:** (K38, P48) twice. Rep this patt for 12" from PU row. Cut MC.
- **Dec rnd:** *With CC, K38, (P3tog) 16 times,* rep from * to * once—108 sts.
- With size 11 needle, purl 4 rnds. BO pw.

Flap

- With size 15 needle and 2 strands of MC, PU 38 sts from third purl row of back.
- Work 11 rows in St st, keeping first 2 sts and last 2 sts in garter st.
- **Dec rows:** Dec 1 st at each end, inside garter sts, EOR twice.
- Knit 2 rows. BO.

Handle

With 2 strands of CC, make 3 pieces of 4-st I-cord, each 7" long (see "I-Cord" on page 8).

Finishing

- Attach a D-ring clamp at each side of purse (see "Attaching Rings" on page 10).
- Using 2 strands of CC, whipstitch one end of I-cord to a clamp, the other end to a chain link.
- Attach another I-cord piece to other end of chain, then another chain and I-cord piece. Attach the other end of the final I-cord piece to the other D-ring clamp.
- With 2 strands of MC and 1 strand of Fizz held tog, sc around ends of bag and flap (see "Single Crochet" on page 9). Use the purl sts as a guide.
- Felt bag according to instructions (see "Felting" on pages 5–6). Pinch ruffled ends to keep puffy shape.
- Insert magnetic snaps. Glue buttons to top of flap to cover prongs.

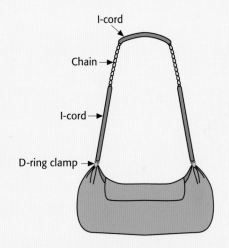

Double Delight

This bag captures the brightness of the sun with a tie-dyed look. The bag's roomy interior is formed by two outer pockets that join smoothly along the sides and bottom.

Materials

- Cascade 220 (100% wool; 220 yards) **4**
  - **MC1** 3 skeins of Yellow (color 4147)
- Cascade 220 (100% wool; 220 yards)
  - **CC1** 2 skeins of Orange (color 7826)
- Di.Ve' Black Jack (100% polyamide; 76 yards) **3**
  - **CC2** 1 ball of Black Jack (color 266)
- Nature Wool (100% wool; 240 yards) **4**
  - **MC2** 3 skeins of Tie-Dyed Yellow (color 37)

- Size 15 US (10 mm) circular needle (29")
- Stitch holders
- Stitch marker
- Assorted yellow and orange beads, ¼" to ½" diameter
- 1 pair of 8½" acrylic ring handles
- 1 skein of size 5 yellow perle cotton and embroidery needle

Skill Level: Intermediate

Finished Size after Felting:
Approx 16" wide x 10½" high x 2" deep

Note: *Beg bag at top. Work 2 strands of yarn held tog throughout unless otherwise indicated.*

Bag Sides (Make 2)

- With 2 strands of CC1 and 1 strand of CC2, CO 90 sts. Join into round, PM. Work rev St st for 5 rnds. Cut yarns.
- **Inc rnd:** Using 1 strand of MC1 and 1 strand of MC2 held tog, (K8, inc in next st) around— 100 sts.
- Work St st for 18".
- **Join bottom:** Divide sts in half. Knit sts from front needle tog with sts from back needle; don't bind off. Put rem 50 sts on holder.

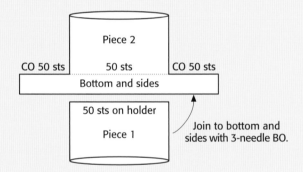

Bag Bottom

- With 2 strands of CC1, CO 50 sts, knit across 50 sts from first side, use needle CO to CO 50 sts— 150 sts (see "Needle Cast On" on page 9).
- Work 7 rows of St st.
- **Join second side:** BO 50 sts kw, knit across, turn. BO 50 sts kw, hold second side in front. Join, using 3-needle BO (see "Three-Needle Bind Off" on page 8).
- Whipstitch side panels to both sides of bag.

Finishing

- Felt bag according to instructions (see "Felting" on pages 5–6).
- **Sew handles:** Wrap top of purse over handles and whipstitch with perle cotton to inside under purl rows.
- Attach beads to sides of bag with a running stitch, using perle cotton and placing 3 to 4 beads on each stitch.

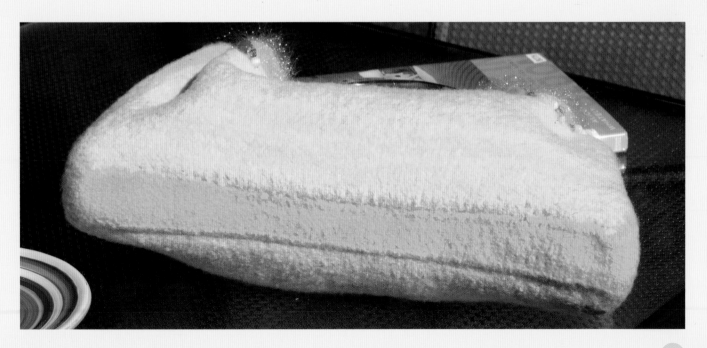

Strictly Business

Even serious business attire doesn't have to be too serious. This chic bag works for the office or an afternoon out in the sun.

Materials

- Cascade 220 (100% wool; 220 yards) **4**
  - **MC**   3 skeins of Coral (color 7830)
  - **CC**   1 skein of Sage Green (color 9410)
- Size 15 US (10 mm) circular needle (24")
- Size 11 US (8 mm) circular needle (24")

- Size 13 US (9 mm) double-pointed needles
- Stitch markers
- 1 magnet-button closure
- Perle cotton or embroidery floss and embroidery needle
- Tapestry needle

Skill Level: Intermediate

Finished Size after Felting: Approx 13" wide at bottom, 11" wide at top x 10½" high

Note: *Beg bag at top. Work 2 strands of yarn held tog throughout.*

Bag

- With size 11 needle and 2 strands of CC, CO 90 sts. Join into rnd, PM. Purl 1 rnd.
- Cut CC and add MC.
- With size 15 needle, knit for 5". Mark first and 46th stitch.
- **Inc rnd:** (Knit to marked st, M1, sl marker, K1, M1) twice—94 sts.
- Knit for 5"
- **Inc rnd:** (Knit to marked st, M1, sl marker, K1, M1) twice—98 sts.
- Work for 17" from CO. Cut MC, add CC, and knit 1 row.
- Join bottom with 3-needle BO (see "Three-Needle Bind Off" on page 8).

Flap

- With size 15 needle and 2 strands of MC, PU 45 sts at back of purse from CO edge.
- Keeping 2 sts at each end in garter st, work St st for 16 rows, ending with RS row.

- **Shape flap:** K2, P6, K5, P19, K5, P6, K2. **Next row:** Knit. **Next row:** K8, BO 5, K18, BO 5, K7.
- Finish each section separately. Work 4 rows in St st, keeping 2 sts at each end in garter st. End with 4 rows of garter st. BO.

Handles (Make 2)

- With dpn and 2 strands of CC, CO 6 sts. Knit 1 row. Beg with knit row, work 6 rows in St st, keeping 1 st at each end in garter st.
- **Dec row:** K1, (K2tog) twice, K1. Do not turn— 4 sts.
- Cont working 4 st I-cord for 20" (see "I-Cord" on page 8). Turn.
- **Inc row:** P1, inc in next 2 sts, P1—6 sts.
- Work 6 rows in St st, keeping 1 st at each end in garter st. Knit 1 row. BO kw.

Pocket

- With size 15 needle and 2 strands of MC, CO 24 sts. Work St st for 7", keeping 2 sts at each end in garter st.
- Switch to size 11 needle, drop both strands of MC, and add 2 strands of CC, knit 1 row. BO kw.

Finishing

- With 2 strands of CC, whipstitch along sides of bag, around flap, and around pocket. With 2 strands of MC, whipstitch around handle base and along handle strap.
- Felt bag, handles, and pocket according to instructions (see "Felting" on pages 5–6).
- Sew handles on bag to fit into openings.
- Using perle cotton or embroidery floss, sew pocket to front of bag and magnet-button closure to flap.

Capri

Is it time for vacation yet? This funky bag always makes me think of the Italian Riviera.

Materials

- Cascade 220 (100% wool; 220 yards)
    - **A** 2 skeins of Blue (color 7607)
    - **B** 2 skeins of Pink (color 7608)
    - **C** 2 skeins of Green (color 7601)
    - **D** 2 skeins of Yellow (color 7600)
    - **E** 2 skeins of Orange (color 7824)

- Size 15 US (10 mm) circular needle (24")
- Size 11 US (8 mm) double-pointed needles
- Size J/10 (6 mm) crochet hook
- 1 pair of rattan handles, 5½" x 11¼"
- Perle cotton or embroidery floss and embroidery needle

Skill Level: Easy

Finished Measurements after Felting:
Approx 11½" wide x 13" high x 4" deep

Note: *This bag is worked sideways with 2 strands of yarn held tog throughout. To change to a different color, cut the 2 strands you're using, pick up 2 strands of the next color, and start knitting with both strands.*

Bag

- With size 15 needle and A, CO 50 sts.
- *Knit 6 rows in St st.
- Using B, knit 2 rows of garter st.
- Using A, knit 2 rows of garter st. Cut A.
- Using B, knit 6 rows of St st.
- Using C, knit 2 rows of garter st.
- Using B, knit 2 rows of garter st. Cut B.
- Using C, knit 6 rows of St st.
- Using D, knit 2 rows of garter st.
- Using C, knit 2 rows of garter st. Cut C.
- Using D, knit 6 rows of St st.
- Using A, knit 2 rows of garter st.
- Using D, knit 2 rows of garter st. Cut D.*
- Rep from * to * 4 times total. BO sts kw. Join BO to the CO for side seam (see grafting BO sts to CO end in "I-Cord" on page 8).

Bottom
With size 15 needle and 2 strands of E, PU 38 sts along front (6 wide stripes) and work 26 rows in garter st. BO.

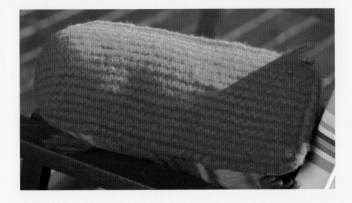

Top Edge
With size 15 needle and 2 strands of E, PU 114 sts around top. Purl 3 rnds. BO pw.

I-Cord Ties (Make 10)

Make 2 ties of each color.
With dpn and 2 strands of yarn, CO 3 sts. Work 3-st I-cord for 9" (see "I-Cord" on page 8).

Inside Pocket

- With size 15 needle and 2 strands of C, CO 40 sts. Work St st for 13".
- **Dec row:** (K8, K2tog) across—36 sts. Change to 2 strands of B and knit 6 rows. BO kw.

Finishing

- **Sew bottom to bag:** Match 6 stripes for back and 2 stripes for sides. Sc with 2 strands of E around bottom (see "Single Crochet" on page 9).
- Insert handle ties through garter ridges on top and tie a knot in each one.
- **Attach fringe to garter ridges:** For fringe, cut yarn in 7" lengths and fold in half. Pull loops through with crochet hook and then slip open ends through loop. Refer to photo of completed bag for placement.
- Felt bag and pocket according to instructions (see "Felting" on pages 5–6).
- Tie I-cords to handle, using double knots, while bag is still damp. The knots can be pulled tighter while the bag is still damp.
- Sew pocket inside after all pieces are dry (see "Seams" on page 11).

Carmen

Think of Spain, flamenco, and black lace. The beaded handle adds a touch of class to this dressy bag.

Materials

- Cascade 220 (100% wool; 220 yards) **4**
    - **MC** 3 skeins of Hot Pink (color 7802)
    - **CC1** 1 skein of Magenta (7803)
    - **CC2** 1 skein of Black (8555)
- K1C2 Sprinkles (60% poly, 40% viscose; 190 yards) **2**
    - **CC3** 1 skein of Magenta (color 220)
- Size 15 US (10 mm) circular needle (24")

- Size 11 US (6 mm) needles
- Stitch markers
- 1 pair of black bead handles, 15" long
- 1 large hook and eye
- 1 black purse closure
- Sewing needle and thread

Skill Level: Experienced

Finished size after Felting:
Approx 12" wide x 10" high x 4½" deep

Note: *Beg bag at bottom. Work 2 strands of yarn held tog throughout unless otherwise indicated.*

Bag

- With size 15 needle and 2 strands of CC1, CO 36 sts. Work rev St st for 24 rows. Cut yarn.
- With CC2, PU 24 sts from a short end, PU 36 sts from next long side, PU 24 sts from next short end, K36—120 sts. Purl 1 rnd. Cut CC2.
- Add MC, knit 4 rnds.
- **Dec rnd:** (K24, PM, K1, K2tog tbl, K30, K2tog, K1, PM) twice—116 sts. Knit 1 rnd. Work 2 more dec rnds EOR (dec after first marker and before second marker)—108 sts.
- Knit even until piece measures 8½" from PU edge.
- **Dec rnd:** (K24, sl marker, K3, K2tog, knit to within 5 sts of next marker, K2tog tbl, K3, sl marker) twice—104 sts. Knit 1 rnd.
- **Dec rnd:** (K24, sl marker, K2, K2tog, knit to within 4 sts of next marker, K2tog tbl, K2, sl marker) twice—100 sts. Knit 1 rnd.
- **Dec rnd:** (K24, sl marker, K1, K2tog, knit to within 3 sts of next marker, K2tog tbl, K1, sl marker) twice—96 sts. Knit 1 rnd.
- Add 1 strand of CC3 to MC, knit 4 rnds.
- Divide sts in half for front and back: K12, turn. P48, turn.
- **Dec:** K11, K2tog, K22, SSK, K11, turn—46 sts. Purl 1 row. K10, K2tog, K22, SSK, K10, turn—44 sts. Purl 1 row. Cont dec until 26 sts rem.
- With WS facing, join yarn to other side and work second side same as first, starting with P48.

Top Trim

- With size 15 needle, 2 strands of CC2, and RS facing, PU 18 sts starting from bottom of side opening, PU 24 sts from top, PU 18 sts down other side. Use needle CO to CO 5 sts (see "Needle Cast On" on page 9). Knit across all the sts, then use needle CO to CO 5 sts.
- Work 4 rows rev St st. BO pw. Rep for other side.

Strap Closure

- With size 15 needle, RS facing, and 2 strands of CC2, PU 12 sts from middle of first purl row of back. Work rev St st for 5".
- **Dec row:** K3, K2tog, K2, K2tog, K3—10 sts. Cont rev St st for 4". BO.

Embellishment Piece

After this piece is felted, you can cut it into strips and sew it to the bag to accentuate the bag's classic shape. With size 11 needles and 1 strand of CC2, CO 30 sts. Work St st for 19".

Inside Pocket

With size 11 needles and 1 strand of MC, CO 50 sts. Work St st for 11". End with 4 rows in 1 strand of CC1. BO.

Finishing

- Felt bag, embellishment piece, and pocket according to instructions (see "Felting" on pages 5–6).
- Insert handles at top of bag below trim.
- To make accent strips, cut embellishment piece in strips ¾" wide. Attach strips to bag with sewing thread, along front and back, using a backstitch and the photo as a guide.
- Sew pocket inside bag.
- Sew hook-and-eye closure inside top trim. Sew strap closure to end of strap and front of bag.

Lagoon

This bag started with two beautiful buttons. The movie The Blue Lagoon *gave me the name. Let the yarn and buttons you have inspire you.*

Materials

- Cascade 220 (100% wool; 220 yards) **4**
    - **MC** 2 skeins of Jade (color 7812)
    - **CC** 1 skein of Turquoise (color 7919)
- Size 15 US (10 mm) circular needle (24")
- Size 13 US (9 mm) circular needle (24")

- Size 13 US (9 mm) double-pointed needles
- Stitch marker
- 2 buttons, 1" diameter
- Tapestry needle

Skill Level: Beginner

Finished Size after Felting:
Approx 10" wide x 9" high x 3" deep

Note: *Beg bag at bottom. Work 2 strands of yarn held tog throughout.*

Bag

- With size 15 needle and 2 strands of CC, CO 30 sts. Work 14 rows in St st, ending with a knit row.
- PU 10 sts from a short end, PU 30 sts from next long side, PU 10 sts from next short end, PM—80 sts. Knit 5 rnds.
- Cut CC. Add MC and knit until piece measures 16" from PU rnd.
- **Dec rnd:** (K6, K2 tog) around—72 sts.
- Drop MC, add CC. With size 13 circular needle, knit 1 rnd. BO pw.

Flap

- With size 15 needle and 2 strands of MC, PU 15 sts from center back along BO edge. Keeping the first 2 sts and last 2 sts in garter st, work St st for 8".
- **Dec rows:** Dec 1 st at each end, inside garter sts, EOR 4 times—7 sts.
- **Next row:** K2, K3tog, K2—5 sts. Knit 2 rows. BO kw.

Flap Tie

Using size 13 dpn and 2 strands of CC, work 3-st I-cord for 12" (see "I-Cord" on page 8).

Handles (Make 2)

- With size 13 dpn and 2 strands of CC, CO 4 sts. Knit 3 rows. Drop both strands of CC and add 2 strands of MC.
- **Dec row:** K1, K2tog, K1—3 sts. Do not turn. Cont working I-cord for 18".
- **Inc row:** K1, inc 1, K1—4 sts. Cut both strands of MC and add 2 strands of CC. Knit 3 rows. BO kw.

Finishing

- Sew handles to top edges, beg from each corner.
- Work a running st with 2 strands of CC up each corner and along the handles. The sts create a finished, cordlike edge on the corner and handles.
- Whipstitch around flap with 2 strands of CC.
- Felt bag and flap tie according to instructions (see "Felting" on pages 5–6).
- Make holes for flap tie by pushing a knitting needle in and out of front of bag, leaving a space for flap between. Push flap tie through holes.
- Sew on buttons, using photo of finished bag as a guide.

Iris

Fall is almost here, and bulbs will soon be planted, but we are not letting summer go without having some fun. The beadwork is easy but impressive.

Materials

- Cascade 220 (100% wool; 220 yards) **(4)**
    - **MC**   4 skeins of Purple (color 7808)
    - **CC**   1 skein of Dark Plum (color 8886)
- Size 15 US (10 mm) circular needle (29")
- Size 13 US (9 mm) circular needle (29")
- Size 11 US (8 mm) needles
- Stitch marker
- Grommet kit and hammer

- 2 square grommets, ½"
- 4 gold heavy-duty snaps
- 1 separating zipper, 22", by Riri, color Rio
- 1 bag of black pony (4 mm) beads
- Sewing needle and thread to match zipper
- 4 purse feet
- Perle cotton or embroidery floss and embroidery needle

Skill Level: Experienced

Finished Size after Felting:
Approx 10½" wide x 9" high x 6½" deep

Note: *Beg bag at bottom. Work 2 strands of yarn held tog throughout unless otherwise indicated.*

Bag

- With size 15 needle and 2 strands of CC, CO 40 sts. Knit 1 row.
- Beg with a knit row, work St st for 24 rows, keeping 2 sts at each end in garter st.
- Knit 2 rows.
- PU 24 sts from a short end, PU 40 sts from next side, PU 24 sts from next short end, PM—128 sts. Purl 1 rnd. Cut CC.
- Add MC, and work in patt (K40, P24) twice for 4 rnds.
- On the next rnd and every following fifth rnd, add beads to the 40 sts on each side as follows: (Add a bead, K4) 8 times. Move beads 1 st to left on bead rnds. For example, the next bead rnd would read: K1, (add a bead, K4) 7 times, add a bead, K3 (see "Adding Beads to a Bag" on page 10).
- Work in patt for 9" from the PU rnd.

Pocket Openings

- With size 15 needle, *K40, drop (do not cut) both strands of MC, add 2 strands of CC, and with size 13 needle K24, turn. BO 24 sts kw.
- Cut both strands of CC and pick up 2 strands of MC. With size 15 needle, use needle CO to CO 20 sts (see "Needle Cast On" on page 9).* Rep from * to * once—120 sts.
- Cont in rnds, knitting all sts, adding beads every fifth rnd as before, until piece measures 14" from PU rnd.
- **Work short rows:** K65, *turn, sl 1, P29, turn, sl 1, K24, turn, sl 1, P19, turn, sl 1, K14, turn, sl 1, P9, turn, sl 1.* Knit to 5 sts past marker, rep from * to * once.
- Knit around all sts, M1 before each sl st, then knit the M1 st tog with sl st.
- **Dec rnd:** (K8, K2tog) around—108 sts.
- Cut both strands of MC and add 2 strands of CC, knit 1 rnd, purl 1 rnd. BO pw.

Pocket Flaps

- With right sides facing, size 15 needle, and 2 strands of MC, PU 22 sts from CO sts. Work St st for 12 rows, keeping first 2 sts and last 2 sts in garter st.
- Dec 1 st at each end EOR, inside garter sts, 3 times—16 sts. Knit 3 rows. BO kw.

Pocket Linings

With size 15 needle and 2 strands of CC, PU 20 sts from under flap. Work St st for 9". BO.

Strap

- With size 11 needles and 1 strand of MC, CO 3 sts. Knit, inc in first 2 sts, K1—5 sts.
- Work St st, keeping 1 st at each end in garter st, for 30".
- **Dec:** K2tog, K2tog, K1. BO.

Finishing

- Felt bag and strap according to instructions (see "Felting" on pages 5–6).
- After bag is dry, sew pocket linings to inside of bag with perle cotton or floss.
- Insert square grommets to top ends of bag to thread handles through. Follow manufacturer's directions to insert grommets.
- Attach snaps to handle strap and pockets, following manufacturer's instructions.
- Sew in zipper at top with the sewing needle and thread.

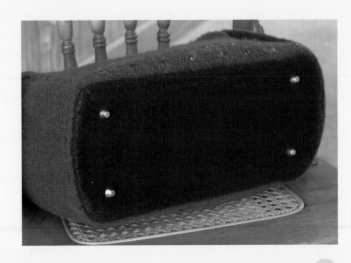

All in One

This bag is quick and easy to make. An optional felted flower adds a special touch.

Materials

- Cascade 220 (100% wool; 220 yards) **4**
    - **MC** 2 skeins of Gray (color 8400)
    - **CC1** 1 skein of Magenta (color 7803)
- Crystal Palace Fizz (100% poly; 120 yards) **4**
    - **CC2** 1 skein of Magenta (color 7225)

- Size 15 US (10 mm) circular needle (24")
- Stitch marker
- **Optional:** Felted flowers (see "Felted Flowers" on pages 12–13)

Skill Level: Beginner

Finished Size after Felting: 13½" wide x 11½" high

Note: *Beg bag at top. Work 2 strands of yarn held tog throughout unless otherwise indicated.*

Bag

- With 2 strands of MC, CO 90 sts. Join into rnd, PM. Purl 1 rnd, knit 1 rnd, purl 1 rnd.
- Change to CC1, knit 1 rnd, purl 1 rnd.
- **Handles:** K10, make opening for handles, referring to "One-Row Buttonholes" on page 8 and working BO 25 sts and CO 25 sts, K20, BO 25 sts and CO 25 sts as before, K10.
- Add 1 strand of CC2 to the 2 strands of CC1 and knit 1 rnd, purl 1 rnd.

- Cut both strands of CC1 and add 2 strands of MC to the 1 strand of CC2, knit 4 rnds. Cut CC2.
- Cont with 2 strands of MC until piece measures 15" from beg.
- Add 1 strand of CC2 to the 2 strands of MC. Knit 4 rnds.
- Drop both strands of MC and add 2 strands of CC1. Knit 4 rnds. Cut CC2 and cont with 2 strands of CC1, knit 4 rnds.
- Join bottom with 3-needle BO (see "Three-Needle Bind Off" on page 8).

Finishing

- Felt bag according to instructions (see "Felting" on pages 5–6). Pull on the handle to form the shape.
- **Optional:** Make flowers (see "Felted Flowers" on pages 12–13) and pin them to the bag.

Mrs. Watson

Doctor Watson and Sherlock Holmes will be joining us shortly. Lots of pockets can be discovered in this bag.

Materials

- Cascade 220 (100% wool; 220 yards) **[4]**
    - **MC1** 1 skein of White Tweed (color 7628)
    - **CC1** 1 skein of Burgundy (color 2401)
    - **CC2** 1 skein of Turquoise (color 8891)
- Noro Kureyon (100% wool; 109 yards) **[4]**
    - **MC2** 2 skeins of color 90
- Size 15 US (10 mm) circular needle (24")
- Size 13 US (9 mm) needles

- Size 11 US (8 mm) double-pointed needles
- Stitch holders
- Stitch marker
- 4 silver crimps
- 2 silver snaps
- 1 zipper to match top flap, 10" long
- Sewing needle and thread to match zipper
- Perle cotton or embroidery floss and embroidery needle

Skill Level: Experienced

Finished Size after Felting:
Approx 12½" wide x 7" high x 3" deep

Note: *Beg bag at bottom. Work 2 strands of yarn held tog throughout unless otherwise indicated.*

Basket Pattern

Wyib, slip all sts pw.
Rnd 1: With 1 strand of MC2, (K3, sl 1) around.
Rnd 2: With MC2, (P3, sl 1) around.
Rnd 3: With 2 strands of MC1, knit.
Rnd 4: With MC2, K1 (sl 1, K3) around, end with K2.
Rnd 5: With MC2, P1 (sl 1, P3) around, end with P2.
Rnd 6: With MC1, knit.

Bag

- With size 15 needle and 2 strands of CC1, use provisional CO to CO 15 sts (see "Provisional Cast On" on page 9). Work St st for 40 rows. Place these 15 sts on holder.
- With MC1, *PU 40 sts from long side of bottom, use needle CO to CO 16 sts, PU 40 sts from next long side, use needle CO to CO 16 sts, PM—112 sts. (see "Needle Cast On" on page 9). **Purl 1 rnd.**

- Work in Basket patt until piece measures 9" from PU row. Make sure you end on a knit row using MC1.

Pocket Openings
- Knit 4 sts, *K13, turn, K13, turn. Referring to "One-Row Buttonholes" on page 8, BO 13 sts and CO 13 sts,* K6, rep from * to * once, knit to end.
- Cont 12 more rows in Basket patt.

Top of Bag
- **Dec rnd:** Cut MC1 and MC2 and add 2 strands of CC2. (K5, K2tog) around—96 sts. P34, BO 14 sts pw, P34 and put these 34 sts on holder, BO 14 sts pw.
- Cont on 34 sts. Work St st for 6 rows, keeping first 2 sts and last 2 sts in garter st. BO pw.
- Join CC2 to sts on holder and work as above.

Pocket Flaps (Make 2)

With RS facing, size 15 needle, and 2 strands of CC1, PU 14 sts from CO sts. Work 6 rows in St st. BO kw, decreasing 1 st at each end.

Pocket Linings (Make 2)

With size 11 dpn and 1 strand of CC2, CO 26 sts. Work St st for 6". BO.

Bottom Flaps

Remove spare yarn from provisional CO. With size 15 needle and 2 strands of CC1, knit 3 rows. Cont in St st (dec 1 st at each end EOR) 3 times—9 sts. BO pw. Work other end the same.

Handle

With size 13 needle and 2 strands of CC1, CO 5 sts. Sl 1 kw wyib, K4, turn. Sl 1 pw wyib, P4, turn. Rep these 2 rows for 28". BO.

Handle Loops (Make 2) and Ties

- With size 11 dpn and 2 strands of CC2, work 3-st I-cord for 6" (see "I-Cord" on page 8).
- Make another long piece of I-cord (about 2 yards) for ties.

Finishing

- Sew ends of bottom seam only. Leave bottom flaps open; you'll sew these after felting.
- Insert handle loops through top of bag close to flaps. Fold handle ends around loops and stitch tog.
- Felt bag, ties, and pocket linings according to instructions (see "Felting" on pages 5–6).
- Cut tie in half after felting and lace through side of bag. Attach crimps to ends.
- Sew pocket linings to inside.
- Attach snaps to pocket flaps.
- Sew in zipper with the sewing needle and thread.
- Sew up bottom flaps.

Designer Bag

Every girl should own at least one classic bag. A designer bag inspired the shape, and the button inspired the colors. The hidden pockets add a touch of practicality to this stylish bag.

Materials

- Cascade 220 (100% wool; 220 yards) **(4)**
    - **MC** 3 skeins of Petrol (color 2404)
    - **CC1** 1 skein of Orange (color 7824)
    - **CC2** 1 skein of Dark Red (color 9404)
    - **CC3** 1 skein of Green (color 2409)
- Size 15 US (10 mm) circular needle (24")
- Size 13 US (9 mm) needles

- Size 11 US (8 mm) double-pointed needles
- Stitch holder
- Stitch marker
- 1 button, 1¼" square
- 1 magnetic snap
- Perle cotton or embroidery floss and embroidery needle

Finished Size after Felting:
Approx 11" wide x 8" high x 4" deep

Note: *Beg bag at bottom. Work 2 strands of yarn held tog throughout unless otherwise indicated.*

Bag

- With size 15 needle and 2 strands of MC, CO 36 sts. Knit 1 row. Work in St st, beg with a knit row, for 6". Keep first 2 sts and last 2 sts in garter st.
- Knit 2 rows.
- PU 16 sts from a short end, PU 36 sts from next long side, PU 16 sts from next short end, K36, PM—104 sts.
- Knit for 9" from PU row.
- **Divide sts in half:** Place half of sts on holder. K8, turn, K2, P48, K2, turn. Keep first 2 sts and last 2 sts in garter st—52 sts.
- **Dec row:** *(K2, SSK, knit to last 4 sts, K2tog, K2) EOR 5 times—42 sts.
- **Next row:** Keeping first 2 sts and last 2 sts in garter st, purl across row.
- **Dec row:** K3 (K2tog, K4) 6 times, end K3—36 sts.
- Knit 3 rows. BO kw.*
- With right sides facing, join yarn to other side. Knit 1 row, purl 1 row, keeping the 2 side sts in garter st.

Flap

- With size 15 needle and 2 strands of CC3, PU 30 sts from center back. Knit 1 row. Cut yarn.
- Add 2 strands of MC. Work 20 rows in St st, keeping first 2 sts and last 2 sts in garter st throughout flap.
- **Dec row:** (K2, SSK, knit to last 4 sts, K2tog, K2) EOR twice—26 sts. Purl on alternate rows keeping first 2 sts and last 2 sts in garter st.
- **Next RS row:** BO 8 sts pw, knit across, turn. BO 8 sts kw, purl to last 2 sts, K2—10 sts.
- Work 6 rows in St st on rem 10 sts.
- **Dec row:** K2, SSK, K2, K2tog, K2—8 sts.

- **Next row:** K2, P4, K2.
- **Dec row:** K2, SSK, K2tog, K2—6 sts.
- BO kw.

Top Trim

With size 15 needle and 2 strands of CC3, PU 30 sts along front edge. Knit 1 row. BO kw.

Handle (Make 1)

With size 13 needles and 2 strands of CC2, CO 7 sts. *K4, sl 3 wyif, turn.* Rep from * to * for 65". BO.

I-Cord Trims (Make 2)

With size 11 dpn and 1 strand of CC3, work 3-st I-cord for 28" to trim flap. Rep with CC1 for 42" to trim bottom.

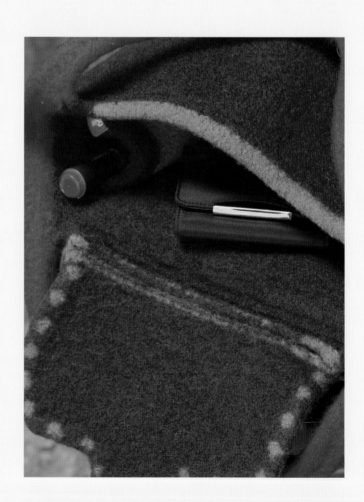

Inside Pockets (Make 2)

Make 1 pocket using CC1 and 1 pocket using CC3.
With size 15 needle and 2 strands of yarn, CO 16 sts.
Work St st for 7". End with 4 rows of garter st. BO.
The sample bag was made with 1 green pocket and 1
orange pocket, each trimmed in blue garter st.

Finishing

• Weave I-cords in and out around flap and bottom,
  going under 2 sts and over 2 sts.
• **Sew on handle:** Starting at top back, whipstitch
  handle sideways along side opening as illustrated
  at right. Then join ends tog, fold handle in half to
  determine middle, and whipstitch other side of
  handle, placing it at bottom of side opening.
• Felt bag and pockets according to instructions (see
  "Felting" on pages 5–6).
• Attach magnetic snap, placing washer on underside
  of flap. Sew large button to front of flap.

• Sew pockets to each end inside the bag so each
  pocket can be accessed from outside without opening the bag.

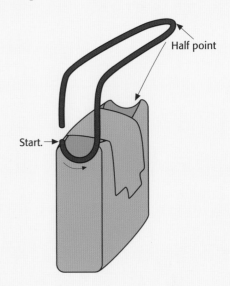

Pony Express

Here's a modern version of an old saddlebag, but you don't need a horse to own this one.

Materials

- Cascade 220 (100% wool; 220 yards) [4]
  - **MC** 3 skeins of Taupe (color 8013)
  - **CC** 2 skeins of Light Taupe (color 8012)
- Size 15 US (10 mm) circular needle (24")
- Size 11 US (8 mm) circular needle (24")
- Size 13 US (9 mm) needles
- Stitch holder

- Stitch marker
- 1 bag of Bag Smith Feathers, color Dark Brown
- 1 adjustable silver buckle set, 1⅛" x 2¼"
- 1 ball of brown leather ribbon, ¼" wide
- 1 oval button, 1" long
- Tapestry needle
- Sewing needle and thread

Skill Level: Intermediate

Finished Size after Felting:
Approx 12" wide x 9" high x 3½" deep

Note: *Beg bag at top. Work 2 strands of yarn held tog throughout unless otherwise indicated.*

Bag

- With size 11 needle and CC, CO 70 sts, join into rnd, PM. Work rev St st for 4 rnds.
- **Dec rnd:** (K5, K2tog) around—60 sts.
- Cut CC. Change to size 15 needle and MC, inc by knitting in front and back of each st—120 sts.
- **Start patt:** (P10, K50) twice. Work in patt for 7".
- **Dec rnd:** (P10, K1, SSK, knit to last 3 sts before next purl section, K2tog, K1) twice—116 sts. Work 3 rnds even.
- **Dec rnd:** (P10, K1, SSK, knit to last 3 sts before next purl section, K2tog, K1) twice—112 sts. Work 3 rnds even.
- **Dec rnd:** (P10, K1, SSK, knit to last 3 sts before next purl section, K2tog, K1) twice—108 sts. Work 2 rnds even.
- **Dec rnd:** (P10, K1, SSK, knit to last 3 sts before next purl section, K2tog, K1) twice—104 sts. Work 2 rnds even.
- **Next 10 rnds:** (P10, K1, SSK, knit to last 3 sts before next purl section, K2tog, K1) twice, decreasing 4 sts each round—64 sts at end of 10th rnd.

Bottom

P10, BO 22 sts, P10 (put stitches on holder), BO 22 sts. Work in rev St st on next 10 sts for 19 rows. Join with kitchener st to rem 10 sts left on holder (see "Kitchener Stitch" on page 8). Whipstitch bottom seams (see "Seams" on page 11).

Flap

- With RS facing, size 15 needle, and 2 strands of CC, PU 30 sts from third purl row in back. Work 3 rows in St st, keeping first 2 sts and last 2 sts in garter st.

- **Inc row:** K2, M1, knit to last 2 sts, M1, K2.
- Cont in est patt, increasing 2 sts every 4 rows 3 more times—38 sts. Work 3" even.
- **Dec row:** Dec 1 st at each end (2 sts in) every 4 rows 4 times—30 sts. Knit 2 rows. BO kw.

Shoulder Straps (Make 2)

- With size 13 needles and 1 strand of MC, CO 6 sts. Work St st, keeping first st and last st in garter st. Make 1 piece 32" long and 1 piece 10" long.
- Sew short strap to left side of bag and long strap to right side of bag at top row of side sts.

Finishing

- Felt bag according to instructions (see "Felting" on pages 5–6). To prevent the flat handle from curling in, check and straighten the handle often during the felting process.
- Whipstitch leather ribbon around flap edges.
- Make a chain loop at center for the button.
- Attach feathers to flap with sewing needle and thread.
- Fasten buckle to straps according to manufacturer's instructions.
- Sew on button at bottom edge in front.

Jackie O

This stylish bag recalls an era of high style and sophistication. My customers took one look and called it Jackie O.

Materials

- Cascade 220 (100% wool; 220 yards) **4**
  - **MC** 2 skeins of Black (color 8555)
- Muench Naturwolle (100% wool; 110 yards) **5**
  - **CC** 1 skein of Yellow/Gray (color 92)
- Size 15 US (10 mm) circular needle (24")
- Size 13 US (9 mm) needles
- Size 11 US (8 mm) needles

- Stitch marker
- 2 black nickel D rings, ¾"
- 1 black nickel swivel ring, ⅜"
- Perle cotton or embroidery floss and embroidery needle
- **Optional:** 1 magnetic snap
- **Optional:** 1 felted flower (see "Felted Flowers" on pages 12–13)

Skill Level: Easy

Finished Size after Felting:
Approx 10" wide x 7½" high x 4" deep

Note: *Beg bag at bottom. Work 2 strands of yarn held tog throughout unless otherwise indicated.*

Slip-Stitch Pattern

Wyib, sl all sts pw.
Rnd 1: With 2 strands of MC, knit.
Rnd 2: With 1 strand of CC, (sl 1, K3) around.
Rnd 3: With 2 strands of MC, knit.
Rnd 4: With 1 strand of CC, K1, (sl 1, K3) to last 2 sts, K2.

Bag

- With size 15 needle and 2 strands of MC, CO 30 sts. Knit 1 row.
- Work 20 rows in St st, beg with knit row.
- Knit 1 row.
- PU 20 sts from a short end, PU 30 sts from next long side, PU 20 sts from next short end, K30, PM—100 sts. Add CC. Work slip-stitch patt in rnds until bag measures 13" from PU row. Cut CC.
- **Dec rnd:** With MC, (K8, K2tog) around—90 sts.
- **Attach D rings:** P4, purl next 10 sts through ring, P35, purl next 10 sts through ring, P31. Purl 3 rnds. BO pw. See "Attaching Rings" on page 10.

Flap

- With size 15 needle and 2 strands of MC, PU 27 sts from second purl row in back.
- Keeping first 2 sts and last 2 sts in garter stitch, work St st for 6".
- **Dec:** Dec 1 st at each end EOR, inside garter sts, 3 times—21 sts.
- Knit 2 rows. BO kw.

Handle

- With size 13 needles and 2 strands of MC, CO 5 sts. Work St st for 36". The handle is knit flat and allowed to roll into a rounded edge during felting.

- Attach one end to D ring and other end to swivel ring, using 1 strand of MC. The handle can be worn long or short.

Inside Pocket

With size 11 needles and 1 strand of MC, CO 40 sts. Work St st for 9". BO.

Finishing

- Felt bag and pocket according to instructions (see "Felting" on pages 5–6). While felting the bag, fold corners tog underneath D rings to help maintain shape of bag. When it's dry, the bag stays the way you've shaped it.
- Sew pocket inside the bag with perle cotton or floss.
- **Optional:** Attach magnetic snap to flap and sew a felted flower on top.

FRi - 4 5:30

Roses Are Red

The tweedy red yarn and dramatic large button brings to mind a romantic rose garden and the fragrant scent of roses.

Materials

- Jaeger Natural Fleece (100% wool; 93 yards) **5**
    - **MC** 2 balls of color 527
- Cascade 220 (100% wool; 220 yards) **4**
    - **CC1** 2 skeins of Red (color 9404)
- Trendsetter Aura (100% nylon; 150 yards) **4**
    - **CC2** 1 ball of Red

- Size 15 US (10 mm) circular needle (24")
- Stitch marker
- 1 oval button, 3¼" long
- ¾"-wide black ribbon
- Sewing needle and thread

Skill Level: Beginner

Finished Size after Felting:
Approx 15" wide x 8½" high

Note: Beg bag at top. Work 2 strands of yarn held tog throughout unless otherwise indicated.

Bag

- With 2 strands of CC1, CO 130 sts. Join into rnd. PM. Purl 1 rnd, knit 1 rnd, purl 1 rnd.
- **Handles:** K10, make opening for handles, referring to "One-Row Buttonholes" on page 8 and working BO 45 sts and CO 25 sts, K20, BO 45 sts and CO 25 sts as before, K10. End with 90 sts.
- Purl 1 rnd, knit 1 rnd.
- Cut both strands of CC1. Add 1 strand of MC and 1 strand of CC2, knit 4 rnds. Cut CC2 and cont knitting with 1 strand of MC until piece measures 13" from beg of MC.

- Cut MC and add 2 strands of CC1 held tog with 1 strand of CC2. Work in rev St st for 6 rnds.
- Join bottom with 3-needle BO (see "Three-Needle Bind Off" on page 8).

Flap

With 2 strands of CC1, PU 15 sts from center back. Work 18 rows of garter st. BO.

Finishing

- Felt bag according to instructions (see "Felting" on pages 5–6).
- Sew on button.
- Attach ribbon by pulling both ends through flap, leaving loop for button.
- Tie a bow on top, referring to project photograph for reference.

Crimson

This bag reminds me of an old-fashioned chenille bedspread. It's large enough for a shopping spree.

Materials

- Debbie Bliss Soho (100% wool; 72 yards) **4**
  MC   6 balls of color 37510
- Cascade 220 (100% wool; 220 yards) **4**
  CC1   1 skein of Dark Red (color 9404)
- Crystal Palace Fizz (100% polyester; 120 yards) **4**
  CC2   2 balls of Flame (color 7128)
- Size 15 US (10 mm) circular needle (24")
- Size 11 US (8 mm) circular needle (24")

- Size 13 US (9 mm) needles
- Stitch marker
- 1 pair of red plastic handles, 5" x 6¼"
- 1 button, 1" diameter
- Approx. 16" length of ¼"-wide red velvet ribbon
- Sewing needle and thread
- Tapestry needle

Skill Level: Beginner

Finished Size after Felting:
Approx 19" wide x 10½" high

Note: *Bag is worked from bottom up.*

Bag

- With size 15 needle and 1 strand of MC, CO 50 sts. Join. PM. Knit 1 rnd.
- **Inc rnd:** Knit into front and back of each st around—100 sts.
- **Inc rnd:** (K1, inc in next st) around—150 sts.
- Knit until piece measures 18" from beg. Cut MC.

Top Shaping
With size 11 needle and 2 strands of CC1, K2tog around—75 sts. Purl 3 rnds. BO pw.

Handle Tabs (Make 4)

With size 13 needles and 1 strand of CC1, count 6 sts in from sides, then PU 5 sts from second purl row. Knit for 3". BO.

Top Decoration

- With size 11 needle and 2 strands of CC2, CO 4 sts. Work St st for approx 2½ yards for each side.
- Use a running stitch with 1 strand of CC1 to attach trim to front and back of bag in squiggly waves.

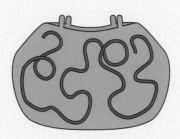

Finishing

- Felt bag according to instructions (see "Felting" on pages 5–6).
- Sew on handles. Fold tabs through opening in the handle and stitch with yarn.
- Sew button to top end.
- Sew ribbon to opposite side with bow tie at the end, leaving a loop for a button closure.

Girls' Night Out

This bag is the perfect size for going to dinner, the movies, or anywhere out with your friends.

Materials

- Cascade 220 (100% wool; 220 yards) **4**
    - **MC**   2 skeins of Blue (color 9457)
    - **CC**   1 skein of Dark Blue (color 8393)
- Size 15 US (10 mm) circular needle (24")
- Size 11 US (8 mm) circular needle (24")
- Size 11 US (8 mm) double-pointed needles

- Stitch marker
- 4 gold purse hooks, 7/8"
- 3 blue-and-gold magnet buttons
- 4 crimps
- Sewing needle and thread

Skill Level: Easy

Finished Size after Felting:
Approx 12½" wide x 6" high x 2½" deep

Note: *Beg bag at bottom. Work 2 strands of yarn held tog throughout unless otherwise indicated.*

Bag

- With size 15 needle and 2 strands of CC, CO 80 sts and join into round. PM. Knit 1 round.
- **Inc rnd:** (Inc in next 3 sts by knitting in front and back of each st, K37) twice—86 sts. Knit 1 rnd.
- **Inc rnd:** K1, inc in next 4 sts, K39, inc in next 4 sts, K38—94 sts.
- Cut CC. Add MC. Knit until piece measures 7" from beg of MC. Drop but don't cut MC.
- Add CC. Work 6 rnds of graph patt (below, right). Cut CC. With MC, knit 4 rnds.
- **Dec rnd:** (K2tog, K6) around, end with K2tog, K4—82 sts.
- Work even until piece measures 12" from beg of MC. Cut MC.
- With size 11 circular needle and CC, purl 3 rnds. BO pw.

Flap

With size 15 needle and 2 strands of MC, PU 24 sts from second purl row of center back. Work 10 rows in St st, keeping first 2 sts and last 2 sts in garter st. Knit 4 rows. BO.

Handles (Make 2)

With size 11 dpn and 1 strand of CC, work 3-st I-cord for 54" (see "I-Cord" on page 8). Weave ends tog to make a circle.

Finishing

- Felt bag and handles according to instructions (see "Felting" on pages 5–6).
- Attach handles with a sling knot to purse hooks.

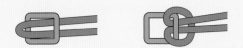

- Poke holes with a metal knitting needle in front and back of bag, close to flap. Slide purse hooks though holes and fasten.
- Sew on magnet buttons at an angle to corners and straight down middle of bag. Refer to project photo for placement.
- Attach crimps. Join the 2 loops of each handle tog one-third of way up length of handle. There are 2 crimps on each handle.

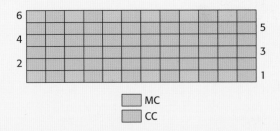

☐ MC
☐ CC

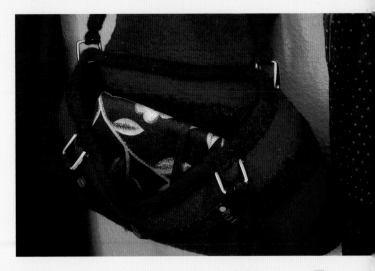

Polar Bear

This cute little bag would be perfect for a winter bride.

Materials

- Cascade 220 (100% wool; 220 yards) **4**
  - **MC** 2 skeins of White (color 8505)
- On Line Smash Irisee (95% poly, 5% Lurex; 90 yards) **4**
  - **CC** 1 ball of White (color 085)
- Size 13 US (9 mm) circular needle (24")

- Stitch marker
- 1 pair of metal D handles, 4½" x 4½"
- 2 magnetic or snap closures for top of purse
- Perle cotton or embroidery floss and embroidery needle
- Sewing needle and thread

Skill Level: Intermediate

Finished size After Felting:
Approx 7" wide x 6" high x 3" deep

Note: *Beg bag at bottom. Work 2 strands of yarn held tog throughout unless otherwise indicated.*

Bag

- Using 2 strands of MC, CO 25 sts. Knit 2 rows. (Purl 1 row, knit 1 row) 3 times.
- PU 8 sts from a short end, PU 25 sts from next long side, PU 8 sts from next short end, PM—66 sts.
- Purl 1 rnd. Add 1 strand of CC and knit 7".
- **Pocket openings:** K5, *drop CC, K15, turn, BO 15 sts, pick up CC. With 2 strands of MC and 1 strand of CC, use needle CO to CO 15 sts,* K18 (see "Needle Cast On" on page 9). Rep from * to *, end K13.
- Cont in rnds until piece measures 8" from beg. Cut CC. Purl 3 rnds. BO pw.

Top Flaps

- With 2 strands of MC, PU 25 sts from last row before the 3 purl rows *inside* of bag.
- Work 5 rows in St st, keeping first 2 sts and last 2 sts in garter st. BO pw.
- Join 2 strands of MC to other side and PU 25 sts from last row before the 3 purl rows *inside* of bag.
- Work 5 rows in St st, keeping first 2 sts and last 2 sts in garter st. BO pw.

Pocket Linings (Make 2)

With RS facing and 2 strands of MC, PU 15 sts from CO edge of pocket opening. Work 5" in St st. BO.

Finishing

- Felt bag according to instructions (see "Felting" on pages 5–6).

  Note: *Felting anything in white requires patience. It takes longer to felt white than any other color. Dunk the bag in ice water between felting sessions. The ice-water dunk will help the bag to felt faster.*

- Sew handles under top purl rows.
- Sew snaps to top with sewing needle and thread.
- Sew pocket linings inside bag.

Black-Tie Affair

Here's a clutch that can go to a party or a show without feeling "under-dressed."

Materials

- Cascade 220 (100% wool; 220 yards) 🧶4
    MC 2 skeins of Black (color 8555)
- Knit One, Crochet Too Sprinkles (60% polyester, 40% viscose; 190 yards) 🧶2
    CC1 1 skein of Black (color 900)
- Katia Gatsby (77% viscose, 15% polyamide, 8% polyester; 115 yards) 🧶3
    CC2 1 ball of Silver Metallic (color 500)
- Size 15 US (10 mm) circular needle (24")

- Size 11 US (8 mm) circular needle (24")
- Stitch marker
- 2 large black nickel plastic O rings, 2" diameter
- 15" length of 1½"-wide black and silver bead trim
- 2 pieces, each 13" long, of black boning
- Sewing needle and thread
- 2 black snaps, ½" diameter
- Tapestry needle

Skill Level: Easy

Finished Size after Felting: 16" wide x 7" high

Note: *Beg bag at top. Work 2 strands of yarn held tog throughout unless otherwise indicated.*

Bag

- With size 11 needle and 2 strands of MC, CO 90 sts. Join into rnd. PM. Purl 1 rnd.
- Drop 1 strand of MC and add 1 strand of CC1. With size 15 needle, knit for 5½".
- **Fold line:** Drop the strand of MC and add another strand of CC1, then knit 1 rnd. This fold line lets the top of the bag fold over smoothly to create a flap on the bag.
- Cut both strands of CC1. Using size 11 needle and 2 strands of MC, knit 1 rnd.
- Change to size 15 needle and knit 2 rnds.
- **Attach O rings:** (K39, knit next 6 sts though ring) twice (see "Attaching Rings" on page 10).
- Knit in rnds until piece measures 16" from beg.
- Purl 3 rnds. Join bottom seam with 3-needle BO (see "Three-Needle Bind Off" on page 8).

Vertical Stripes

With 2 strands of CC2 and a tapestry needle, work a running stitch, going under 2 rows and over 2 rows. Start at bottom, 4 sts from sides, and space stripes 2 sts apart. Weave snugly to keep accent sts from looping. Refer to photo for placement.

Strap

With size 11 needle, 1 strand of MC, and 1 strand of CC1, CO 4 sts. Work St st for 20". BO.

Finishing

- Felt bag and strap according to instructions (see "Felting" on pages 5–6).
- Attach snaps to strap ends and attach to ring when wanted. Remove when not needed.
- Sew boning material inside, underneath fold line.
- Fold top of bag over to one side to create a flap. Sew bead trim to edge of flap, referring to photo for placement.

Cosmetics Pouch

Nothing is handier than having all your cosmetics neatly stored in one place. And with this lovely bag, you always have a mirror handy.

Materials

- Cascade 220 (100% wool; 220 yards) [4]
  - **MC** 1 skein of Blue (color 7607)
  - **CC1** 1 skein of Pink (color 7608)
  - **CC2** 1 skein of Yellow (color 7600)
- Size 11 US (8 mm) circular needle (16")
- Size 10½ US (6½ mm) circular needle (16")

- Stitch marker
- 1 mirror, 3" square
- 1 zipper, 8" long
- Sewing needle and thread
- Perle cotton or embroidery floss and embroidery needle

Skill Level: Easy

Finished Size after Felting:
8¼" wide x 5" high x 1½" deep

Note: *Most of the bag is worked with 1 strand of yarn. Two strands are used at beg and end of bag as noted in patt.*

Pouch

- With size 11 needle and 2 strands of MC, CO 40 sts. Drop 1 strand of MC and work 11 rows in St st. Add 1 strand of MC and purl 1 row. Drop 1 strand of MC and cont with 1 strand only.
- PU 8 sts from a short end, PU 40 sts from next side, PU 8 sts from next short end, K40, PM—96 sts. Cont working in rnds.
- Purl 1 rnd.
- **Work stripes:** Knit 1 rnd with MC, 1 rnd with CC1, 2 rnds with MC, 2 rnds with CC1, 3 rnds with MC, 3 rnds with CC1, and 4 rnds with MC. Cut MC. Knit with CC1 until piece measures 7½" from beg. Cut CC1.
- **Dec rnd:** With size 10½ needle and MC, (K6, K2tog) around—84 sts.
- Purl 3 rnds. BO.

Inside Pocket

With size 11 needle and 1 strand of CC2, CO 60 sts. Work 4" in St st. Knit 2 rows. BO.

Mirror Pocket

With size 11 needle and 1 strand of CC1, CO 20 sts. Work 7" of St st in stripes (2 rows each with CC1 and CC2). BO.

Finishing

- Felt pieces according to instructions (see "Felting" on pages 5–6). While felting the bag, fold top corners down to give pouch more personality. When it's dry, the bag stays the way you've shaped it.
- Cut mirror pocket to size approx ¼" larger than mirror. Cut opening for mirror, leaving a frame of 1".
- Sew pocket to front of pouch with a needle and sewing thread, using a backstitch. Leave top open so you can slide mirror in. The space behind mirror is perfect for an ID card.
- Turn pouch inside out. Sew inside pocket. Carefully backstitch vertical dividers, leaving a space for lipstick or other items you carry.
- Sew in zipper only along top. Leave the upper corners pushed in to create an interesting shape at the top of the bag.

Eyeglasses Case

This lovely case makes even a pair of plain reading glasses seem stylish and beautiful.

Materials

- Cascade 220 (100% wool; 220 yards) **4**
  1 skein of Medium Pink (color 9478)
- Size 11 US (8 mm) circular needle (16")
- Size 10 US (6 mm) circular needle (16")
- Size 11 US (8 mm) double-pointed needles

- Stitch marker
- 1 rhinestone buckle (1" diameter)
- Small magnetic snap
- Small piece of pink bias tape
- Sewing needle and thread

Skill Level: Easy

Finished Size after Felting:
Approx 6½" wide inside case x 3" high

Note: *Beg case at bottom. Work with 1 strand of yarn throughout.*

Case

- With size 11 circular needle, CO 74 sts. Join into rnd, PM. Purl 3 rnds.
- Work patt (P4, K33) twice. Cont in est patt until piece measures 3¾" from beg.
- Shape top by changing to size 10 needle and purl 3 rnds. BO 41 sts pw.

Flap

With size 11 circular needle and 1 strand of yarn, work St st on rem 33 sts, keeping first 2 sts and last 2 sts in garter st. When flap measures 1H", ending with WS row, *BO 4 sts at beg of next 2 rows. Work 2 of rows St st.* Rep from * to * 3 times total. BO pw.

Handle

Using size 11 dpn and 1 strand of yarn, CO 4 sts. Work rev St st I-cord for 15" (see "I-Cord" on page 8).

Finishing

- Sew bottom seam.
- Turn piece WS out. On each side, tuck the 4 knit sts toward the inside of the case to make a pleat. Whipstitch along the edge of the knit sts. Turn case RS out to reveal I-cord type of edging at the sides.
- Sew handle to top of sides.
- CO 6 sts and knit 10 rows St st to create a small piece of fabric to serve as a tab for the buckle. Felt this tab along with case.
- Felt bag according to instructions (see "Felting" on pages 5–6).

Note: *Stuff case with paper after felting to keep the shape rounded and pinch sides to reinforce side trim.*

- Attach magnetic snap.
- Cut a tie shape, approximately 2" long, from extra felted fabric you made. Weave into buckle and sew the tab on top to cover back of snap.
- Sew a small piece of bias tape inside to cover snap prongs. This protects the glasses from being scratched when they are placed inside the case.

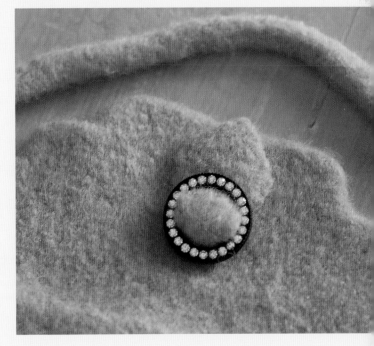

Cell Phone Holder

This is a great companion for the Purple Haze bag on page 20. With its swivel hook, this holder easily attaches to the handle of any purse. Make one in each color to match your wardrobe.

Materials

- Cascade 220 (100% wool; 220 yards) **4**
  - **MC** 1 skein of Purple (color 8888)
- Small amounts of 2 contrasting colors for trim: Dark Purple (color 8886) and Lavender (color 7809). You'll need less than 10 yards of these contrasting colors.
- Size 11 US (8 mm) circular needle (16")

- Stitch marker
- 2 small D rings, 1¼"
- 1 small swivel hook
- 1 magnetic snap
- Sewing needle and thread

Skill Level: Beginner

Finished Size after Felting:
Approx 3½" wide x 4" high x 1" deep

Note: *Beg holder at bottom. Work with 1 strand of Cascade throughout.*

Holder

- With 1 strand of MC, CO 20 sts and work 8 rows in rev St st, beg with knit row.
- PU 6 sts from a short end, PU 20 sts from next side, PU 6 sts from next short end, PM—52 sts.
- Work in patt (K20, P6) twice. Work until piece measures 7" from PU rnd.
- **Dec rnd:** P20, P4, P2tog, (P3, P2 tog) 4 times, P4, P2tog—46 sts.
- **Attach D rings:** P20, purl next 5 sts through ring, P16, purl next 5 sts though ring (see "Attaching Rings" on page 10).
- Purl 2 rnds. P20, BO 26 sts pw—20 sts.

Flap

- Cont on rem 20 sts in St st , keeping first 2 sts and last 2 sts in garter st until flap measures 2½".
- Dec 1 st at each end EOR twice. Knit 2 rows. BO.

Handle

CO 4 sts. Work St st for 18". BO.

Trim

- With RS facing and the Dark Purple contrasting color, PU 62 sts along last knit st before 6 purl sts, beg from top, around bottom, and up other side. BO kw. Rep for other side.
- To make a decorative heart, use the Lavender contrasting color to CO 12 sts and knit 12 rows in St st. BO.

Finishing

- Using 1 strand of MC, sew 1 end of handle to D ring and other end to swivel hook.
- Felt bag and trim according to instructions (see "Felting" on pages 5–6).
- Attach magnetic snap. Cut out heart shape from lavender trim piece and sew with blanket st on top of flap to cover snap prongs.

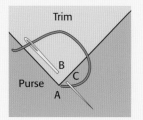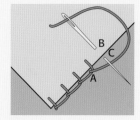

Blanket stitch

Abbreviations

approx	approximately		psso	pass slipped stitch over
beg	begin, beginning		PU	pick up and knit
BO	bind off		pw	purlwise
CC	contrasting color		rem	remain, remaining
CO	cast on		rep	repeat
cont	continue		rev St st	reverse stockinette stitch
dec	decrease		rnd	round
dpn	double-pointed needles		RS	right side(s)
EOR	every other row		sc	single crochet
est	established		sl	slip
inc	increase		SSK	slip 1 knitwise, slip 1 knitwise, knit these 2 stitches together through the back loops.
K	knit			
K2tog	knit 2 stitches together			
kw	knitwise		st(s)	stitch(es)
M1	make 1 stitch		St st	stockinette stitch
MC	main color		tbl	through back loop
mm	millimeter(s)		tog	together
P	purl		WS	wrong side(s)
P2tog	purl 2 stitches together		wyib	with yarn in back
patt	pattern		wyif	with yarn in front
PM	place marker			

YARN WEIGHTS

Yarn-Weight Symbol and Category Names	**1** Super Fine	**2** Fine	**3** Light	**4** Medium	**5** Bulky	**6** Super Bulky
Types of Yarns in Category	Sock, Fingering, Baby	Sport, Baby	DK, Light Worsted	Worsted, Afghan, Aran	Chunky, Craft, Rug	Bulky, Roving

YARN CONVERSIONS

Yards x .91 = meters

Meters x 1.09 = yards

Grams x .0352 = ounces

Ounces x 28.35 = grams

Resources

Contact the following distributors to find a retail store near you.

Beadland
www.beadland.com
Pure Allure Crystal Innovations magnetic clasps

Bryson Distributing
www.brysonknits.com
Magnets, buckles, and rings: Clover; Eucalan

Cascade Yarns
www.cascadeyarns.com
Cascade 220, Kid Seta: Madil, Black Jack: Di.Ve'

Crystal Palace Yarns
www.straw.com
Fizz, Fizz Stardust

Euro Yarns
www.euroyarns.com
Smash Irisee: On Line

Ann Geddes Studio
www.geddesstudio.com
Buttons

Knit One, Crochet Too, Inc.
www.KnitOneCrochetToo.com
Sprinkles

Knitting Fever
www.knittingfever.com
Nature Wool, Soho: Debbie Bliss, Gatsby: Fil_Katia, Kureyon: Noro

M & J Trimming
www.mjtrim.com
Rhinestone buckles, purse closures, handles

Muench Yarns
www.muenchyarns.com
Naturwolle, buttons, magnet buttons

Pure Allure, Inc.
Email: pajewelry@aol.com
Crystal Accents closures

RiRi
www.JudithAnneLtd.com
Zippers

Sunbelt Fastener Co.
www.SunbeltFashion.com
Purse handles, snaps, hooks, chains, rhinestone buckles

Westminster Fibers, Inc.
Email: info@westminsterfibers.com
Natural Fleece, Jaeger

Or contact the author directly:
Eva's Needlework
1321 E. Thousand Oaks Blvd.
Thousand Oaks, CA 91362
805-379-0722

About the Author

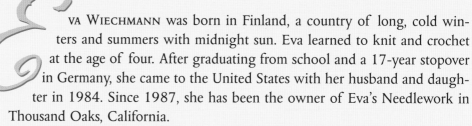

EVA WIECHMANN was born in Finland, a country of long, cold winters and summers with midnight sun. Eva learned to knit and crochet at the age of four. After graduating from school and a 17-year stopover in Germany, she came to the United States with her husband and daughter in 1984. Since 1987, she has been the owner of Eva's Needlework in Thousand Oaks, California.

At Eva's shop, every knitter and needleworker can feel at home. The excitement is contagious when you walk into this store packed with yarn. Eva's Needlework was featured in a knitting publication as one of America's premiere shops, which made Eva and her loyal customers very proud. In addition, one of her designs has been published by Classic Elite.

Also by Eva: *Pursenalities* (Martingale & Company, 2004).